Rabbit Punch!

GREG SANTOS

Rabbit Punch!

LIVRES
DC
BOOKS

Cover art by Katy Lemay.
Author photograph by Studio Duda.
Book designed and typeset by Primeau Barey, Montreal.
Edited by Jason Camlot.

Legal Deposit, Bibliothèque et Archives nationales du Québec
and Library and Archives Canada, 1st trimester, 2014.

Library and Archives Canada Cataloguing in Publication
Santos, Greg, 1981- , author
Rabbit punch!/Greg Santos.
Poems.
ISBN 978-1-927599-23-5 (bound).–ISBN 978-1-927599-22-8 (pbk.)
I. Title.
PS8637.A584R32 2014 C811'.6 C2014-901286-1

For our publishing activities, DC Books gratefully acknowledges the financial support of the Canada Council for the Arts, of SODEC, and of the Government of Canada through Canadian Heritage and the Canada Book Fund.

Canada Council for the Arts Conseil des Arts du Canada

Société de développement des entreprises culturelles Québec

Printed and bound in Canada.
Interior pages printed on Enviro Book, an environmentally responsible paper containing 100 % post-consumer recycled fiber, processed chlorine-free and manufactured using biogas energy.
Distributed by Fitzhenry and Whiteside.

DC Books
PO Box 666, Station Saint-Laurent
Montreal, Quebec H4L 4V9
www.dcbooks.ca

In Memory of Paul Violi

Contents

!

!!

!!!

!

For we were made to reach for things.
For imagination extends life.
For our reach must exceed our grasp.

–Paul Violi,
"For It Feels Like February 29th or 30th"

Our Seafaring Ways

There is an ocean waiting to be swum.
If you wish to swim it, hold my hand.

We will struggle through the portending fog
portending a magnificent storm.

Picture yourself bobbing amidst foam and froth.
Zoom out farther. What do you see?

Spiderwebs, labyrinths, constellations.

In the New Republic of Poetry

after Martin Espada

Poets scrawl their verses onto knives,
flinging cutlery into the air,
letting chance decide.

Gypsies slink through throngs,
slipping scrolls of poems
into oblivious purses and pockets.

And the hungry can slip into a bordello
and be fed poems until ink
drips down their chins.

We have returned to this good land,
where the forest at twilight
is filled with the mingling cries
of wolves and flying baboons.

Lullaby

A little way ahead
winter is come

Do you remember
it ever being so cold?

Ash trees burn
above white paths

The sky goes on
with cool indifference

Wheels of the train
fall silent

We have arrived
at the junction

All creatures
don their coats

A little way ahead
winter is come

Hansel and Gretel

Mother and Father warned us not to go beyond the valley.

We went searching for you deep in the woods.

We were coaxed by promises of peppermint, floss, doom.

The thought of catching a glimpse of your fingernails
excited and scared us.

We were ready to die for love.

We heard your voice calling us despite all the
wind machines.

We couldn't stop ourselves from stumbling through
the brambles.

Scraped knees, wet socks, burs wedged in our hair.

Dandelions like jellyfish swarming our ankles.

We heard the muffled screech of an owl somewhere
far away.

At long last, love in all its glory.

Cronus

The farmer has a basketful of eggs.
He wonders if he should bring them back to their coop.
But they are his children and he is hungry.

On the Night Train

Motionless in my seat
I chase the moon.
Streaks of street lamps
appear and recede.
The glow of floating windows
offer guilty glimpses
of Punch and Judy shows.

Trees reach up with twisted fingers
furiously trying to scratch out the face
of the man in the moon,
succeeding briefly when we pass
a patch of woods,
but at a clearing he reappears:
a slice of white refusing to be erased.

We Were Startled by the Sound of Fog

an erasure from Out of the Fog by C. K. Ober

The wind sprang and finally sounded so near,
it seemed we could almost see our hearts.

We heard the whistle of thought,
but she quickly passed us,
too far away to see or hear.

The sounds grew fainter
and soon we were alone again.

It was bitter, this companionship,
for we were perishing,
yet in too great of a hurry to stop.

The Prodigal Son

That feeling the executioner has
when he hangs up his mask at the end of the work day,
I have that right now.
Like a rabbit punch out of the blue.
I feel on kilter and that worries me.
But I'm not complaining.
I'm just singing a requiem for all decent centaurs
everywhere.
The digital photo frames of the present
do not compare to the daguerreotypes of the past.
Take a bayonet to the face
and you regret it for the rest of your life.
It's best not to dwell.
I say it's better to pack one's bindle
and hobo it down to the freight yard.
That way you won't feel like a permanent intern
and that elephant you've had on your back all your life
will be off scratching its back on a tree in some open field.
Skulking back into the village
long after they've forgotten they tarred and feathered you,
the prodigal son will be welcomed home with loving arms.

Abyss

Picture an anglerfish shuddering
in its sleep in the murky deep of the sea.

It has never even seen the sun.

The Cave

She slowly opens her eyes,
observing the ash swirl under the moonlight.

She reaches behind her head, unclips her mask,
and breathes very slowly.

He is asleep, his frame rising and falling as he breathes.
At least we're breathing, she thinks.

Tiny Elephants

A girl cups a handful of tiny elephants.
When they trumpet all at once
they sound like a tiny kazoo.
In effect, they are musical chickpeas.

The Green Bike

A child's green bike propped up against a white picket fence. A yellow Volkswagen Beetle idling in the driveway. A battalion of green toy soldiers strewn upon the lawn. An empty red Radio Flyer on its side. A rainbow of flowers and wreaths lined up by the front door. A lone American flag saluting.

Of Squirrels and Elephants

One squirrel carries another,
lifeless, in its mouth.
Paws, slipping, struggle up a tree.

Watching this creature and its burden,
I think of elephants,
gently touching the skulls, tusks
of their kin with their trunks, feet.

And I wonder if we might find,
nestled among the branches of elms,
tiny bones, ancient treetop cemeteries.

The Game

June. Afternoon. They march toward the baseball
  diamond.
The sun is sinking. Risk of thunderstorms.

A gray wind disturbs the trees.
In the leaves, butterflies kneel in prayer.

Prayer for shelter, wings in spasms
like mouths of saints speaking in tongues. A plea to
  ward off rain.

Still, they march.
Heads bowed, wooden bats nestled and heavy on
  their shoulders.

The procession trudging toward the dusty field.
To play the game before night comes.

Before lampposts lift themselves from the ground,
leaving crumbs of light so the players can find their
  way home.

Tree Frogs

In the summer we caught
frogs while they burped
at the edge of ponds,
their spawn bubbling,
shimmering in the sun.

We were fast,
grabbed them
with bare hands,
squeezed until
they stopped squirming.

Tied string around their bodies,
hung them on pine trees,
left them dangling
all through summer and fall,
waiting for winter to come.

In December,
wearing boots, heavy jackets,
we trudged through
clean snow
till we reached the pines

where we proudly
showed off our
homemade christmas ornaments:
tiny skeletons,
bones tinkling in the wind.

We Laughed Like Drains

We puffed up
our chests and strutted.

We talked
about our hazy
futures and mottled pasts.

We read between
the lines and giggled
like schoolgirls.

Our sides ached
as tears
cursed our faces.

We kept laughing
even when it stopped
being funny.

We couldn't shake
off the eternal fatigue
in our bones.

Can't we stay
like this forever?

Midnight Concerts

Tender strumming drifts from my fish's aquarium, filling the bedroom with an excess of yearning, as if we were trapped in a diamond. At first I was surprised my goldfish could play guitar but soon I came to accept it just as he, in time, welcomed me into his secret audience. Songs of icebergs drifting in open water, groaning, as they glide southward, trailing their robes of white, melting into nothing. Once I made the mistake of asking what his songs meant. Glassy-eyed, he stared, bobbing in the water, and said: "I long for that which is gone."

Mean Boys

Mean boys,
we do not wish you
infamy in death.

May you lie
sleepless
in your holes.

May the echoes
of your angry screams
for attention

from the bottom of wells
go unheard
for the rest of our lives.

La Mue

In late July the voices of cicadas rise, fall,
singing their syncopated songs.

The males try to impress potential mates,
older ones more confident, cocksure.

Freshly moulted and uneasy in their new bodies,
the young sing with wavering voices.

If you look carefully,
you can find their abandoned skins

stuck to bark around the neighbourhood,
still singing to the trees.

It Is Snowing in Paris

Charcoal-roasted chestnuts glow,
incandescent bulbs about to explode.

Wayward snowflakes
rip the heavens like meteors.

Parisians whip open their umbrellas,
force fields to keep meteors at bay.

The snow is terrible but nothing like back home,
where cold locks your soul in a vice.

I store my soul in a fur-lined case
in the boreal forests of Canada.

Reading Ou Yang Hsiu in a Café

There is a flying pig on the mural.
I find this mildly comforting,
as if the cosmos were reminding me
an impossibility had been made possible,
by a viewer like me.
It is a damp autumn afternoon.
The waiters are busy watching soccer on TV
and the impenetrable depth of my espresso is like the
    Loch Ness.
I am lucky. I have no dead friends like Ou Yang Hsiu.
But I have lost friendships over the years.
Some drifted apart like hulking icebergs.
The past is a desolate chunk of Greenland.

Today All I Hear Outside Is Sadness

But last night
was just lovely:
we got caught
in the rain.
Tonight I'll be
in the laundry room.
Why go there?
To be eternal.
I love this city.
It is so old and held
together by magic.

A Versailles of the Mind

It's that time of year again.
Crocuses spring forth
and birds perch on my eyelids.
My history is a little fuzzy.
I think this poem was built
during the time of Louis XIV.
From afar it's all gold and legend,
but up close it's just mortar and dust.
Renovations continue 'til this very day.
Care to join me on my daily strolls
through living sculpture?
The fresh air will do wonders for the heart.
My dears, look closer, this poem
contains small, exquisite topiaries.

Napoleon's Hat

Pacing my hallways
These days I find myself
Dressed as Napoleon

I brush my teeth
Dust off my bicorn
Salute the day

I hum my imperial tune
In the steamy shower
My voice a marching band

The rain outside
Is my adoring throng
O how I miss you

My glorious
France of yore

!!

Must Sean Penn always look like he's squeezing
the last drop out of a sponge and the sponge
is his face? Even the back of his head grimaces.

–Dean Young, "Sean Penn Anti-Ode"

My Beloved

I need you as a seahorse needs the briny sea in which it lives.

Without you, I am utterly lost.

I am like a zombie with no access to human brains, so tasty
and so soft.

I want to live inside you, a baby in the life-sustaining fluid
that is you.

I need you like a chocoholic craves a fix of chocohol.

We need each other like politicians need pundits and
celebrities need paparazzi.

We are like Batman and Robin, Mary Kate and Ashley,
Black and Decker.

Our love cannot be measured or explained by
modern science.

Our love is the Loch Ness Monster.

We will travel the world and taste every exotic potato chip
flavor known to man.

We will have a baby and we will not enter it in
beauty pageants.

We will raise our child to be polite and earnest.

We will teach it to love Weird Al like we do.

When the time comes to discuss the birds and the bees,

I will do my best to clarify that birds *do not* have sex with bees.

Our darling child will in time leave home, find its own beloved to need.

We will grow old together and I shall wear the bottoms of my trousers rolled.

Paris Hilton on Tara Reid

She always seemed like she was having a good time,
you know?
At P. Diddy's party she did Jell-O shots with Nicky on top
of the bar
while Lindsay Lohan regaled partygoers with
a dramatic reading
of "Charge of the Light Brigade" clad only in bed sheets.
It was so hot!

But lately Tara's been crying in public over the
smallest things.
I mean, at the Versace shindig the waterworks
started flowing
just because she lost her dog-eared copy of *The Picture
of Dorian Gray.*
I know she just misplaced it like she always does after
too many drinks.

So guess what she does? She starts reciting "The
Hollow Men."
Talk about a downer... locked herself in the restroom
for three hours!
I tried to cheer her up with "Ode on a Grecian Urn" but
it was no use.
When she finally opened the door, she bumped into
me, whimpering,

"This is the way the world ends. This is the way the
world ends..."
Seriously creeped me out! We really need to find that
girl a boyfriend.

The Harder You Work, the Luckier You Get

When a black cat prowls nearby,
Prime Minister Stephen Harper crosses the street.

With a pocketed loony on his person,
he hangs a horseshoe above his doorway.

He is forever tucking a rabbit's foot
under his hair helmet.

He dons usurped ties from vanquished foes
and keeps, in his heart, a steady mantra:

If Ottawa Giveth, Then Ottawa Can Taketh Away.

Gotham Knight

I am the fog that chokes the air.
The bat that's tangled in your hair.

I hide beneath your bed at night.
I am The Rife, criminals, The Rife.

I am Vengeance. I am Wrath.
I roam the subway with the rats.

I am The Night that you don't see.
Super Man's got nothing on me.

Spider-Man spins a dainty web.
I make bad guys really dead.

Green Lantern's ring makes a pretty light.
I don't do pretty. I do fight.

I taught Charlie Sheen to win.
I chucked Chuck Norris in a bin.

Stallone, Willis, & Van Dam:
All nobodies. I'm the man.

Mike Tyson?
Baddest man on the planet.

I'm like the Death Star.
I blow up planets.

Rhyme planet with planets?
I break the rules.

I am The Batman.
I do what I–KAPOW!

Many years later, as he faced the press junket, McCain was to remember that distant afternoon when his father took him to discover bubblegum ice-cream

John McCain was born on the same day as Michael Jackson.

As a boy, McCain frolicked amid the fragrant hollyhock.

At a Sunday School picnic, McCain was chagrined over the charring of his marshmallow.

On his 13th birthday, McCain was knocked unconscious by a rogue piñata.

Before long, McCain supped upon bowl after bowl of Lucky Charms. Alone.

Sometimes, when no one was looking, McCain cheated at Mad Libs.

Whilst sipping on a mimosa, McCain experienced a frisson before his mother's china hutch.

The next day, McCain leapt across a manhole with marked coolness.

Over time, McCain discovered his hidden talent for shadow puppetry.

At age twenty-eight, McCain eyed his mailbox with unbridled malice.

One evening, McCain awoke in a panic, unsure whether to use Head & Shoulders or Pert Plus.

On Wednesday, McCain was full of woe.

Behind the curtain, McCain gnawed introspectively upon a baby-back rib.

Two days ago, McCain strode confidently towards his expired medication.

At day break, McCain was especially amused at the sight

of the Weather Network.

At 11:47 a.m., McCain recovered his self-possession via Overeaters Anonymous.

At high noon, McCain consumed his penultimate shawarma.

On this fateful day, McCain stood athwart the cheese aisle.

I May Be Macho but I'm no Genius

Reincarnation doesn't have to be.
You can concentrate and you can mental telepathy.
Yeah!
–"Macho Man" Randy Savage

I can't stop thinking about Miss Elizabeth.
My sunglasses do little to hide the pain.
No more Pomp and Circumstance.

I'm more Burger King than Macho King.
I snapped into too many Slim Jims.
I still feel randy all the time but my inner savage is gone.

I may be a Poffo but I no longer feel boffo.
I wouldn't wish Macho Madness on anyone, brother.
I miss Elizabeth.

Marco Polo in Manhattan

Friday was nice.
Friday was nice, and we were friends.
–Elizabeth Bishop, "Crusoe in England"

O Jerry, how I long to return to Xanadu…
I was a young man when I
first met the munificent emperor of the Tartars
and was welcomed with open arms.

I think of its stately pleasure dome.
It was Khan's posh summer home.
A refuge from the strife, warfare, corruption
spreading gangrenous across his sandswept empire.

You know of Xanadu's opulence:
labyrinthine Mongolian magnolia gardens, jade thrones,
objets d'art accumulated from his conquests,
statues, black marble, white marble, a marvel!

Kublai Khan's menagerie, the largest since Noah's:
manic monkeys; zebras; earnest elephants; camels;
    yakety yaks;
blithe birds of paradise; musk deer; petty peacocks; giraffes;
ten thousand flawlessly white horses,

whose milk could be drunk only by the royal family;
felonious falcons; lions; arty albino tigers; wolves;
yes, even doddling dodo birds; blue footed boobies;
and a unicorn enclosure overlooking the river.

But few know of his garden filled with swings,
a merry-go-round, Whack-a-mole, polo,

petoncle, a sandbox the size of an Olympic pool.
O the sandcastles we made and toppled!

O Xanadu!
Always an inviting crash pad!
O the lavish amenities!
O the complimentary yak hair slippers!

The Great Khan was truly a great man.
To those in his closest entourage
he was simply Kublai.
What more can I tell you?

I remember camping out in the royal backyard,
sipping on mojitos, nibbling on spring rolls, curry puffs.
K-Dawg and I tossed yak dung patties like Frisbees.
We told ghost stories and made shadow puppets all night.

I wore my finest Venetian silk pajamas,
Kublai draped in his favorite camel furs.
We sipped on hot cocoa by a blazing fire, set up a yurt,
unfurled our sleeping bags, slept under the starry stars.

You know, I have no idea how I lived so long
without pastrami and corned beef on rye.
I can, at long last, die fulfilled
and give up the ghosts of yesterday.

But Kublai, my dear Kublai, died of gout.
It was his damn fondness for
animal organs, red wine, smoked cheese;
Deli-style chicken liver sandwiches did him in.

Oh, are you going to have that pickle, Jer?

The Mysterious Dr. Ramsey

The Mysterious Dr. Ramsey collects unused air sickness bags for a hobby as one would collect foreign coins. He does not travel by air very often, but receives bags from family and friends who do, especially if they are flying with more exotic airlines. He proudly shows off his panoply of bags from all around the world, of every shape, size, and colour and has dubbed himself the "Noah of Barf Bags." He dreams of opening an air-sickness bag museum called The Mysterious Dr. Ramsey's Sac Museum. "Ugh!" and "Gross!" are common refrains when people learn of his passion but he never falters and is never ashamed. One should be so lucky, to have found one's true calling.

Zombies

Zombies like listening to The Cranberries

Particularly their hit song, "Zombie."

Zombies like the song because they can relate to it.

They nod their heads, mouths agape.

"Ughhhhhhhhh," they grunt affirmatively.

Zombies, however, do not like Rob Zombie.

He is not an authentic zombie.

He is a live human who has appropriated the zombie name.

There is no greater zombie taboo.

Look out, Rob Zombie! Behind you!

Just kidding.

Or am I?

Presidential Address

The president was on TV
and told us all to keep calm.
Nothing's going on.

See, my wife said,
I like the president.
He's not freaking out
like the rest of us.

I turned to my wife.
That man is not
the president,
I said, knowingly.

A Coal Miner on Mars

With red dust on his hands, he slogs around in the carbonate mines and thinks of his wife and spawn. As he chisels and shovels, his mind is elsewhere: he still hasn't gotten around to writing a will, but he'll get around to it one day. He wouldn't want the space courts intervening and costing his family a bionic arm and a leg. After all the anger management classes, he finally feels settled and happy for a change. A sudden and thunderous rumbling jolts him out of his stupor. The pudgy alien next to him yelps, "Sorry about that, Ragnor. I missed lunch and my stomachs have been acting up all day."

The First Birdbrain

While munching on an apple and daydreaming of hydraulic pumps, Leonardo witnessed a falcon dive-bombing a smaller bird and instantly became obsessed with flying.

Soon after, a servant brought Leonardo a steaming bowl of chicken broth and walked into the workshop without knocking. Leonardo darted out the door like a freshly decapitated chicken.

Leonardo spent countless hours whittling little bird figurines and tossing them over his balcony. "Caw caw caw!" he'd often say to bewildered friends and family.

On that fateful winter day in January, he strapped his goggles on and adjusted the leather straps around his shoulders.

"Squawk," he said closing his eyes, stepping off the cliff, and swooping into history; unsuccessfully testing the world's first flying machine.

Brock Lesnar: Here Comes the Pain

Brock Lesnar was raised on a farm in North Dakota.

As a child, Lesnar dodged a barrage of arrows with glee.

Consequently, Lesnar is now unable to eat s'mores without grimacing.

On his 15th birthday, Lesnar hid among the karaoke singers and dreamed of being the next big thing.

Almost immediately, Lesnar witnessed a frightening vision of things to come.

Years later, Lesnar rode blindfolded o'er the eighteenth hole atop a golf cart.

For a few moments a day while sparring, Lesnar pondered why man can't taste his own tongue.

Once, when his wife was out shopping, Lesnar snuck into a Pilates class with marked coolness.

Later that month, Lesnar intervened in a lawsuit on behalf of the girl scouts.

One evening, Lesnar awoke in a cold sweat, racking his brain about how they get the caramel in the Caramilk bar.

Before long, Lesnar lamented the loss of his favourite boyhood futon.

Subsequently, Lesnar could never get the hang of Sudoku again.

Over time, Lesnar spent many days tirelessly checking his number of Facebook friends.

Craving Pop-Tarts after a night on the town, Lesnar came to know the true meaning of loneliness.

Eventually, Lesnar took up collecting novelty Pez dispensers and odd-shaped postcards.

Between bouts, Lesnar spends his time perfecting his uncanny gift for ventriloquism.

After all, Lesnar credits his many championship wins to his unwavering belief in the Tooth Fairy and the Easter Bunny.

A Wild Night at Hooters

If it were up to me, I would convince T. S. Eliot to
skip church,
break Pound out of St. Elizabeth's, drag Yeats away from
Maude Gonne
(she was a bad influence on him anyway); take them all
to Hooters.

We'd get smashed drinking Coors, spot Whitman coming
on to Frost,
we'd have to keep Yeats away from the dartboards,
him and Dylan Thomas would be doing too many
whisky shots.

Eliot would stumble to the jukebox, complain they
didn't have
the Shakespearian Rag, I'd say I thought he didn't like
that song
(when we all knew he really did).

Ted Hughes would spend too long listening to Hemingway
trade war stories
with Wilfred Owen, showing each other their battle scars
à la Jaws,
Sylvia having to send Ted home in a cab.

We'd congregate on the sidewalk after closing time
wondering what to do next,
decide to crash at my place, waking up the next day
with hangovers
(everyone in the mood to eat fried peanut butter, bacon,
banana sandwiches).

An Instruction Manual

Once I dreamed that I could float.

Not fly (let's be realistic here) but you know, hover.

Not only could I float vertically but I could turn myself horizontally in mid-air.

I coasted down flights of stairs, escalators, small hills, with the greatest of ease.

I was so good they gave me the Nobel Prize in Floating.

Be careful not to leave lit candles unattended.

Familiar Phrases

And the room is filled with bugs. Just the way you like it.

Are you done with that yacht?

This thicket is good but not great.

Never mind, he has a hole in his head.

I can understand the Jell-O but why all the rabbits?

That's not a wafer. THIS is a wafer.

I think you've had enough goats' blood for one evening.

What's with you and vomit?

Somebody stop that yak!

Damn it, could you stop decomposing for just a second!

Brrr. Is your brain cold, too?

Which head do you think goes better with this blouse?

Hey, be quiet. The enchanted river's talking again.

Oh, don't mind her. She's just a robot.

If you're not going to the annual human sacrifice,

then I'm not going to be the annual human sacrifice.

What have you got against ogres?

Hey, check out Frank's pantaloons!

Who's up for a siege?

I think a group of knaves attacked him.

Honey, Mr. Lowell is vibrating again.

I want to buy Jeff a pair of pants. How many legs does he have again?

I keep telling you. I'm not a butterfly, I'm a giraffe.

Oh, this old thing? It's a pterodactyl wing.

I now pronounce you mule and mouse.

Long Live the King

after "There Were No Signs," Irving Layton

By Google Mapping I found out
Where I was going.

By being disrespectful to the haters, how to love.
By searching Tumblr, whom and what to reblog.

By texting, how to LOL and ROTFLOL.

Out of image macros, I have built memes.
Out of unlikes, likes.

From hashtags, I have learned to trend.

Almost now I know who I iz.
Almost I have the boosts to be that man.

Another follower
And I shall be the Twitter King.

The Great Hoarder

Sometimes when my wife and kids are asleep
I feel like I am forever filling up an attic
with boxes of knick-knacks I'm not prepared to throw out
but have no clue what to do with.
I think of errands to run: I have to go to the bank,
diaper supplies are dangerously low,
we are out of milk and orange juice...
Other thoughts drift by like odd deep sea fish:
Will I be able to read all the books that are piling up?
My hair is getting too long. Does anyone read my poems?
I wander this dark attic when I cannot sleep,
thinking of friends I've lost touch with
and speak to ghosts in need of company.
They want to know what it's like to be young
and laugh at my talk of being mired with responsibility.
Well, you haven't changed diapers
while trying to write a status update, I say.
You're lucky, I tell them, you don't have to choose
between Apple and Android, Taylor Swift or Miley Cyrus.
Go back to sleep, Greg, they say.
Those are questions for the ages.

!!!

The directions to the lunatic asylum were confusing;
most likely they were the random associations
and confused ramblings of a lunatic.

–James Tate, "Like a Scarf"

Imaginationland

I wander the Tim Burton-ish forest in my head,
the one with the knotted and gnarly trees.

Squirrels dance merrily with foxes
and wind-up owls whirr incessantly.

Every once in a while
my face is whacked by a stray branch–

Honestly, I don't remember ever going outside.
Taxis and ambulances rocket through the thistles.

My family waits for me in a gingerbread house
safely hidden deep in the woods.

This is a weird and wonderful land.
Truly God's country.

We're all Just Passing Strange

for Paul Violi

New York is a little to the left of the centre of the universe.
Everything is happening and I'm so there. Where?
It isn't important to know how but to just do things.

They all make me want to write!
Admittedly, I don't like it when it's just poetry thick.
It needs to be varied.

Suffering from the morning of the poem.
He felt like God writing out the bible.
He connected with their mind set.

He was always "around."
He really lived like a poet.
He was pretty much a ghost.

Epistle to New York

I remember having bad vegetable dumplings with Ben, Alina, Lia, Lauren, and Mollye. The place looked like a rectangle. From the windows it seemed like they only sold trays and cups.

I remember Alina bicycling into a crowd of people, her blue blouse flapping in the crisp autumn evening before disappearing.

I remember walking back from Café Loup with Ben and grabbing cheese fries and hot dogs at Papaya Dog.

I remember going to Papaya Dog one night and being completely flabbergasted by an angry guy who was upset because they wouldn't let his girlfriend use the restroom and he told the cook behind the counter to "Go back to Africa."

I remember we went to the bad dumpling place because someone outside said, "It's good. Really good." And we believed him.

I remember talking about how bad it was to eat greasy late-night snacks, yet still doing it.

I remember having strong coffee and soy milk while sitting cross-legged on Ben's apartment floor.

I remember Ben asking me to buy him some rice crackers and being worried I bought the wrong kind and at the same corner store being asked if I was from India.

I remember having pastrami on rye with Ben at Katz's Deli and feeling both at home and homesick for Schwartz's smoked meat.

I remember walking by beautiful people and people raging mad.

Ghost Hares

Elsewhere referred to as mountain rabbit,
conejo gigantesco, or spirit hopper, the ghost hare
is an enormous, mysterious creature.
An adult male can reach the size of a full-grown cougar.
In the Canadian Rockies, they tend to be a tawny grey.
Ghost hares are shy and typically avoid human contact.
Nevertheless, they have been known to attack cyclists,
lone hikers, careless tourists, and unmonitored
radish leaves.
Never hike alone in areas of known ghost hare sightings.
Keep children close to you.
Never, ever approach a ghost hare,
especially a feeding one, no matter how cute or fluffy
it looks.
Sudden movements might trigger an instinctive attack.
Don't make eye contact.
Don't play dead. And whatever you do, don't act like
a carrot.
Wearing orange around ghost hares is suicidal.

This Poem Wants You to Trust it

Not right away but gradually over time.
It wants to hold hands for a while before getting serious.
It is very patient and understanding that way.
It enjoys making mixtapes to help you get through the work day.
It likes Renaissance fairs, prancing, and enchantment.
It wants to be a guest speaker in your high school gym.
It will come dressed completely covered in glitter.
It will shake itself like a dog and sprinkle its wonderment all over the audience.
It will charm the pants off the crowd.
Some of them will even consider becoming poems themselves when they grow up.
That's just how this poem rolls.
It encourages you to follow the rainbow.
It is the leprechaun of poems.
No, actually it is more like the unicorn of poems.
This poem can only be read
By the pure of heart,
by you.

Titter-Free Existence

I drank rooibos tea today. It tasted
of blood & electric blankets.

The velociraptors are
sleeping in their cots.

The toddlers, stalking
their prey, again.

Today is filled to the brim
with menace & potential.

I started growing out a moustache
& my kids didn't laugh at me.

That is all a dad could ever really hope for.
Not even a titter.

Outside My Window

The elm trees are making a break for it.
The sun has nowhere to go but down.
A glacier shudders.

Children whisper to their water buffalo.
Ripples on a dark lake are all that's left of a struggle.
The dog twitches and growls in its sleep.

A spider senses a tug on its web.
The boarded up corner store has a plank missing.
She wonders briefly if she would still recognize him now.

Eyewear

Eye wake up in a construct.
–Ben Mirov, "Eye, Ghost"

Eye have trouble with my vision.
Eye wear contact lenses and eyeglasses.
Eye still can't see what you see.
Eye have trouble sleeping.
Eye wake up in a sweat.
Eye eat too many starchy snacks at night.
Eye go from bed to couch.
Then from couch to bed.
This can happen five times a night.
Eye turn on the TV and it laughs at me.
Eye linger on The Discovery Channel for too long.
Eye discover nothing and feel empty inside.
Eye can't forget to put the recycling out.
Eye crave grilled cheese sandwiches at inopportune times
Like in the shower or when making love.
Eye turn on the fan when it is too hot.
The oscillating sounds like it's coming from inside my skull.
Eye find this comforting.
Eye can't forget to take the laundry out of the dryer.
Eye don't play sports anymore.
Eye need to watch my waist.
Eye am doing my best to make sense.
Eye get the feeling my TV is watching me.
Eye think my guitar misses me
But I am too shy to return its calls.
Eye don't paint anymore.

Eye think about poetry too much.
There's a fog in my brain only poetry can clear.
Eye can't forget to wring my brain and hang it out to dry.

Brids of a Feather Flock Together

Felt myself reaching for my wallet today.
I was making my regular face.
12 minutes ago I liked something on Facebook.

This poem is confused
due to the misspelling of the word bird.
I learned from Google that 1 billion seconds = 32 years.

I am essentially 1 billion seconds old.
My tabs contain multitudes.
I am a blank search engine.

I am a blinking cursor.
In 1 hour it will be dark & we will be tucked away
in our nests and moaning.

Hooray

Yes, the world
will not have ended in 2012
as the Mayans predicted
but sadly nor will
hoverboards be *en vogue.*
The sun will continue to die,
magnificent tiny creatures
with feelers and luminescent bodies
we've never even discovered
will have gone extinct
under our noses,
but on the plus side
things will be sleeker,
shinier, smaller,
and more expensive.

Oblivion Avenue

When you make the decision to leave
and your loved ones wave their handkerchiefs from
    the docks
like a million mad flappings of Daffy Duck's beak,
you can't help wondering if you've made the right choice.

We leave the shores and drift so all that is left of our past
is an infinitesimal speck on an ancient iceberg,
complaining about its arthritis and bad hips,
melting toward oblivion.

Where? Oblivion Avenue.
You make a left turn at Alburquerque.
Bugs Bunny always made a *wrong toin at Albukoikee*
but he somehow turned out fine. A wrong turn didn't
    stop him.

No. Even with Elmer Fudd at the end of the tunnel,
what didn't shoot Bugs made him stronger. He had the
    right idea.
Burrowing frantically through the dirt
toward a golden carrot that probably never has or ever
    will exist.

We all have an Elmer Fudd waiting for us at our
    final destination,
shotgun in hand, hiding among the welcoming throngs
    on the boardwalk.
Remember, fold your rabbit ears under your bowler hat.
He'll never suspect a thing.

Hatchling

Think of a
happy memory.

Hold on to
that thought
dearly.

It is a
featherslippery thing.

Hold it
as if you
were turning a
newly hatched bird
in your hand.

The hatchling
is a bird of paradise
with magnificent plumage.

See how its beak
glints in the sun?

Meanwhile, What I'm Going to Do

after John Ashbery

How can we stop old wounds from hurting? Protect
yourself now.
Leave behind old routines for your future escapes,
the choices, the goodbyes.

Keep them guarded in a chest for safekeeping.
Lock them away.
Be free to gallop toward dazzling places with names.

We rush down stairs in search of something.
Always falling. How many of us have the injuries
to prove it?

Broken ankles, cracked ribs, shattered femurs,
from sprinting headlong into the unknown, the
unknown that loves us.

Yes, fractures will heal. New skin will stretch over
injured tissue.
But later, 5 years, 10 years, our joints will be
wonderfully swollen, painful.

Types of Silence

after Mark Strand

1

It was the moment before the bread went stale,
before the sleeping dog dreamed of hunting,
the silence before the mantle cracked.

2

The moon had not appeared from behind the clouds,
it was that time of night before the roar of the sun.
Nothing had happened yet.

3

The sea turned away, while a figure was swept out
by the tides.

Love Song

I am a bird
and I love
poets.

They look
so tiny
from up
here.

We the Wild Bunch

after John Ashbery

We knockaround guys.
We shut up and sing.
We big fish.
We take the lead.

We hustle & flow.
We bring it on.
We compañeros!
We walking tall.

We kids in America.
We American outlaws.
We bomb the system.
We starship troopers.

We strangers with candy.
We far from heaven.
We curious, George.
We wordplay.

We pulp fiction.
We stranger than fiction.
We analyze this.
We get smart.

We in the realms of the unreal.
We reign over me.
We duel in the sun.
We get rich or die tryin'.

We walk the line.
We crash.
We war dance.
We ask the dust.

We broken flowers.
We secondhand lions.
We city of ghosts.
We touching the void.

I Don't Have a Status Update for What I'm Feeling

I am too sensitive a creature,
my feelers do their job excessively well.

The Disease Is its Remedy

There is no happiness like mine.
I have been eating poetry.
–Mark Strand, "Eating Poetry"

I have crumbs around the corners of my mouth.
I am a man of Herculean appetites.
I eat poetry like potato chips.

I have been told to vary my diet.
You should indulge in more food groups, they say.
Too much of one thing will give you a stomachache.

But I have a unique condition.
I am prescribed to eat poetry for the rest of my days.
Do not cry for me; it is a happy ailment.

I will round up other inkblot hearts who have
    a taste for salt.
We will pass around books, licking them.
We will whinny and stomp with joy.

This poem has been laced with MSG.
The bag is done.
I can't eat just one.

A Vanishing Act

a lipogram

A magician wows,
yanking rabbits from top hats,
pulling ribbons from his mouth.

Words, such as hocus pocus,
abracadabra: all flash and pizzazz
to distract Jills and Johns. Voilà!

A magician is a conjuror,
dancing, many say,
with spirits, immortality, Satan.

Fog and mirrors,
an illusionist's tools,
and trusting crowds, his fools.

Notes

I gratefully acknowledge the following publications in which poems in *Rabbit Punch!* first appeared:

"Our Seafaring Ways," "Abyss," "An Instruction Manual," "Hatchling," and "We the Wild Bunch" appeared in my e-book *Featherslippery.*

"In the New Republic of Poetry" was inspired by Martin Espada's poem "The Republic of Poetry" and appeared in *Sand: Berlin's English Literary Journal.*

"Lullaby," "Oblivion Avenue," "Meanwhile, What I'm Going To Do," "Types of Silence," and "A Vanishing Act" appeared in my chapbook *Oblivion Avenue.*

"Hansel and Gretel" appeared in *Branch Magazine.*

"On the Night Train" was selected by former Canadian Poet Laureate, Pauline Michel, to appear as a Poem of the Month on the Parliamentary Poet Laureate website.

"We Were Startled by the Sound of Fog" is an erasure poem written using *Out of the Fog* by C. K. Ober as a source text. I used the Erasures website at Wave Books (erasures.wavepoetry.com) to create the found poem. You can make one, too!

"The Prodigal Son" appeared in *My Name is Mud.*

"Tiny Elephants" appeared in the *Elephant Summer* e-book and then in my chapbook *Tweet Tweet Tweet.*

"The Green Bike" first appeared in *6S, The Green Bike Stories.*

"Of Squirrels and Elephants" appeared in *Palimpsest,* Yale University's Graduate Arts and Literary Journal.

"The Game" appeared in *Dingers: Contemporary Baseball Writing.*

"We Laughed like Drains" appeared in *Poets/Artists.*

"Midnight Concerts" appeared in *pax americana.*

"Mean Boys" was originally written as a response to the Virginia Tech Massacre. But then the shootings in Norway happened. And then the Boston Marathon bombing. Countless other atrocities are committed by lost young men every day. It was rewritten as a poem of defiance towards the "mean boys" of the world.

"It is Snowing in Paris," "A Versailles of the Mind," "Imaginationland," "This Poem Wants You to Trust It," "Love Song," "I Don't Have a Status Update for What I'm Feeling," and "The Disease is its Remedy" appeared in my chapbook *Tweet Tweet Tweet.*

"Napoleon's Hat" first appeared in *Her Royal Majesty* and then was republished in my chapbook *Tweet Tweet Tweet.*

"My Beloved" appeared in *Branch Magazine.*

"Paris Hilton on Tara Reid," "Familiar Phrases," and "Ghost Hares" appeared in *The Feathertale Review.*

"The Harder You Work, the Luckier You Get" originally appeared in *Rogue Stimulus: The Stephen Harper Holiday Anthology for a Prorogued Parliament.*

"Gotham Knight" appeared in *The Black Tongue Review.*

"The Mysterious Dr. Ramsey" appeared in *6S, The Mysterious Dr. Ramsey.*

"Zombies" appeared in *New Wave Vomit.*

"Presidential Address" appeared in *Everyday Genius.*

"The First Birdbrain" appeared in *For Every Year.*

"Brock Lesnar: Here Comes the Pain" first appeared in *Finishing Hammers: Mixed Martial Arts Poetry* and then was republished in *The Barnstormer.*

"The Great Hoarder" first appeared on *How Yah Doon?* and was republished in *Daddy Cool.*

"Eyewear" won the 2010 Eyewear Prize for Poetry.

"Hooray" appeared in *This Blog Will Change Your Life.*

"We the Wild Bunch" was inspired by John Ashbery's "They Knew What They Wanted," a poem composed of movie titles.

Acknowledgments

This book would not have been possible without the guidance and support of many, many people.

Rabbit Punch! is dedicated in memory to Paul Violi, whose humour and vibrant spirit helped make my time at Columbia and The New School a life-changing experience. Paul's laughter and our conversations are sorely missed.

Thank you also to my teachers, peers, and friends: David Lehman, Matthew Zapruder, Mark Strand, Dean Young, David McGimpsey, Stuart Ross, Todd Swift, Paula Bohince, Ben Mirov, Alina Gregorian, Mollye Miller, Moe Clark, Jerry Waxman, Joshua Levy, and Ryan Schachter.

Many thanks to my editor Jason Camlot and my publisher Keith Henderson at DC Books for having my back and believing in my writing.

Thank you to my mom, dad, and my loving family. Your unwavering support means the world to me.

To my wife, Maryn, and my children, Rosemary and Arthur, you are my muses. I love you.

Greg Santos is the author of *The Emperor's Sofa* (DC Books, 2010) and the chapbooks *Tweet Tweet Tweet* (Corrupt Press, 2011) and *Oblivion Avenue* (Trainwreck Press, 2008). He holds an MFA in Creative Writing from The New School in Manhattan. He is a poetry editor for the online literary magazine *carte blanche* and teaches the art of verse to at-risk youth. He lives in Montreal with his wife and two children.